WIND AND THE EARTH

NIKKI BUNDEY

Carolrhoda Books, Inc. / Minneapolis

First American edition published in 2001 by
Carolrhoda Books, Inc.

All the words that appear in **bold** type are explained
in the glossary that starts on page 30.

18 / Hutchison Picture Library; Simon Grosset 7 / Impact Photos; Dave Watts
—cover (inset) left / Peter Pickford—title page / Stephen Dalton 5b, 25t
/ Michael Leach 13 / Rich Kirchner 14 / B & C Alexander 17t / John Shaw 19b,
23t / Ralph & Daphne Keller 20b / Eric Soder 25b / Alan Williams 26 / Rod
Planck 27t / NHPA; J.P.Delobelle—cover (inset) right / Norbert Wu 20t / H
Ausloos 23b / Gerard & Margi Moss 24 / John Maier 28 / Mark Edwards 29b /
Still Pictures; 29t / The Stock Market; N Bailey—cover (background) / P
Barkham 5t / H Rogers 9, 19t / B Woods 10 / R.C.Fournier 16 / Richard Blosse
17b / N Bailey 22 / J Ringland 27b / TRIP.

Illustrations by Artistic License/Genny Haines, Tracy Fennell

Carolrhoda Books, Inc.
A division of Lerner Publishing Group
241 First Avenue North
Minneapolis, MN 55401 U.S.A.

Website address: www.lernerbooks.com

A ZOË BOOK

Library of Congress Cataloging-in-Publication Data

Bundey, Nikki, 1948–
     Wind and the earth / by Nikki Bundey
        p. cm. — (The science of weather)
     Includes index.
     Summary: Explains the principles of air movement, air pressure, and seasonal
winds and describes the effects of the wind on landforms, farming, and climate.
        ISBN 1-57505-470-1 (lib. bdg. : alk. paper)
        1. Winds—Juvenile literature. [1. Winds.] I. Title. II. Series: Bundey, Nikki,
1948– The science of weather.
     QC931.4.B84   2001
     551.51'8—dc21   00-023715

Printed in Italy by Grafedit SpA
Bound in the United States of America
1 2 3 4 5 6—OS—06 05 04 03 02 01

CONTENTS

AIR ON THE MOVE

What is air? It looks like empty space, but it is made up of invisible **gases**. The three most important gases are **nitrogen**, **oxygen**, and **carbon dioxide**. They make life on earth possible. The gases form a layer, like a blanket, around our planet. We call the blanket the earth's **atmosphere**.

The atmosphere stretches up into space for about 70 miles. The part of the atmosphere nearest the earth is called the **troposphere**. Here, the air is dusty and often full of clouds.

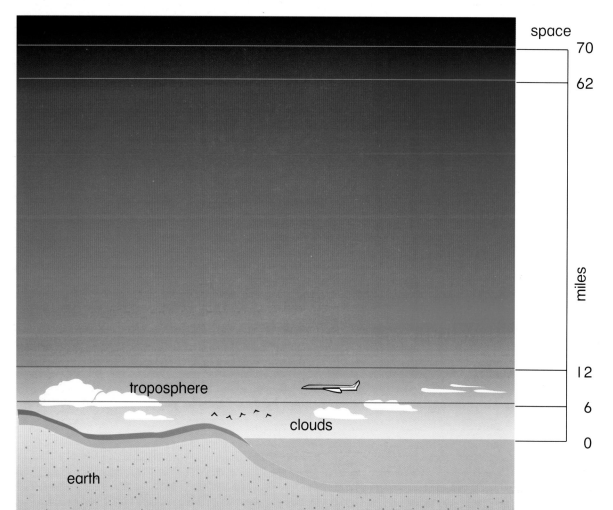

space

70

62

miles

troposphere

12

clouds

6

0

earth

We cannot see the wind in this photograph, but we know it is blowing. It is making the grass move, like waves on the surface of the sea.

Most of the gases lie in the lowest part of the atmosphere, the troposphere. It reaches heights of about five miles above the **poles** and about ten miles above the **equator**.

In the troposphere, air rushes and whirls around the earth. These movements are called air currents, or wind. We cannot see the wind, but we can feel it on our faces and can see what it does.

In northern countries with mild climates, the wind blows dead leaves from the trees each autumn. Winds affect nature and the **environment** in many different ways.

5

WHY DOES WIND BLOW?

Air behaves in different ways at different **temperatures**. For example, when the sun heats the air, the warm air rises. Cooler air then rushes in beneath it. The rushing air is also wind.

During the day, the land warms up more quickly than the ocean. The warm air above the land rises, and cooler air over the sea moves in toward the land, creating a **sea breeze**. The breeze may be felt up to 190 miles inland.

Sea breezes normally blow on warm, sunny days, when the air over the land warms and rises.

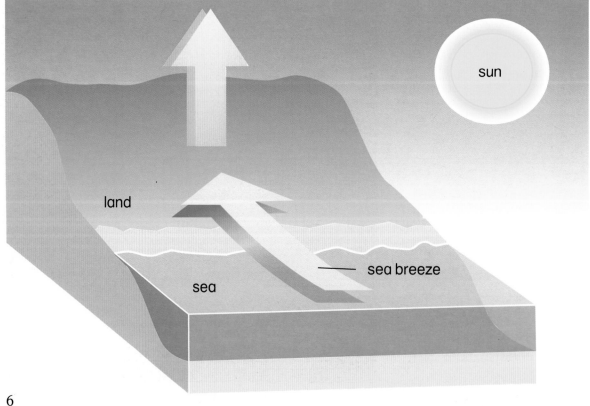

sun

land

sea

sea breeze

Balloons may be filled with gases called hydrogen, helium, or methane. A special burner heats the gases, which rise and carry the balloon upward. In the same way, the warmth of the sun heats air and makes it rise.

At night, the wind blows the other way. The land cools down more quickly than the ocean. The warmer air above the water rises, and air from the land flows back toward the sea, creating a **land breeze**.

The wind pattern switches at night, with a breeze blowing toward the ocean.

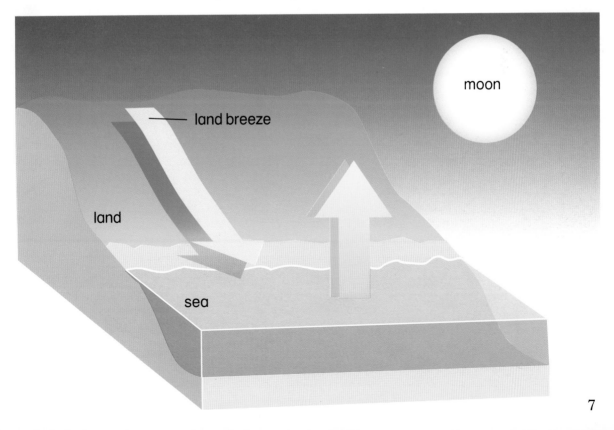

moon

land breeze

land

sea

PRESSURE AND FRONTS

The gases of the atmosphere press down on the surface of the earth. This force is called **air pressure**. Cold, moist air presses down more than warm, dry air. Cold, moist air creates a high-pressure system. Winds in a high-pressure system move in a **clockwise** direction in the northern half of the world. They move counter-clockwise in the southern half of the world. High-pressure systems usually bring clear **weather**, without rain or snow.

On this weather map, lines called **isobars** connect places of equal air pressure. The line with points shows a **cold front** moving in.

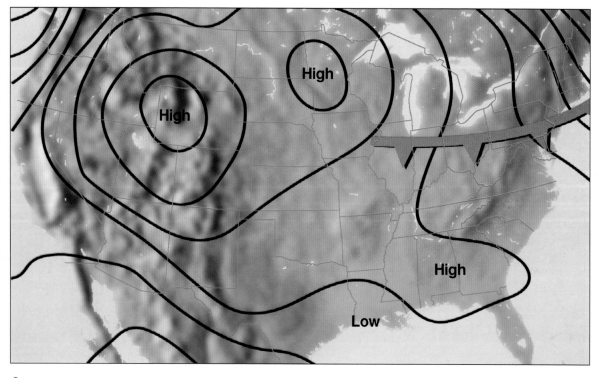

Areas of rising air are called low-pressure systems. As warm air rises and cools, clouds form. Low-pressure systems often bring cloudy, rainy weather. Winds in a low-pressure system move opposite to those in a high-pressure system. The border between a large mass of warm air and a large mass of cold air is called a **front**. Cold fronts bring lower temperatures, and warm fronts bring higher temperatures.

The arrows on this television weather map show strong winds blowing in the British Isles.

THURSDAY 1300

See for Yourself

See how air pressure affects the weather.
- Cut out the weather maps from your newspaper for several weeks. Note whether the maps show low- or high-pressure systems.
- Keep a weather journal over the same period.
- Compare the maps with your journal to learn which pressure systems produce which kinds of weather.

AROUND THE WORLD

About six miles above the earth, long bands of powerful winds circle the planet. They are called **jet streams**.

Nearer to the surface, we feel the **prevailing winds**, the most common winds in each region. Winds are named for the direction from which they blow. For example, the prevailing westerlies blow across North America. They come from the west. Easterly winds blow from the east.

You can tell the direction of the prevailing wind in this picture. The force of the wind has made the tree grow bent.

The North and South Poles are bitterly cold, and the equator is very hot. Because of the difference in temperature, air is constantly moving between the poles and the equator. The earth spins around as it travels in space. The earth's spin twists the paths of the prevailing winds.

The prevailing winds in the northern and southern parts of the world are called westerlies. Easterly winds, called trade winds, blow near the equator. In the days of sailing ships, traders used these winds to sail around the world.

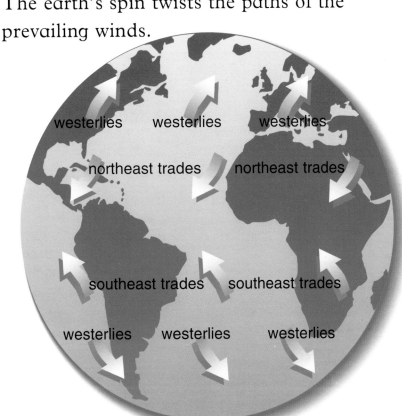

westerlies   westerlies   westerlies

northeast trades   northeast trades

southeast trades   southeast trades

westerlies   westerlies   westerlies

See for Yourself

See how the spinning of the globe affects the wind.
- Hold up a soccer ball. Have a friend point a hair dryer at the center of the ball.
- Can you feel the wind?
- Spin the ball around. Can you feel the wind now?

WATER CARRIERS

One of the invisible gases in the air is **water vapor**. It forms when the sun heats water in lakes and oceans. The water vapor rises high into the atmosphere, where it cools, forming tiny droplets of water. These tiny water droplets make up clouds.

Watch the wind blow clouds across the sky. Often, the water droplets in clouds build up into big drops and fall as rain.

Winds are part of the endless process of rain making that we call the **water cycle**.

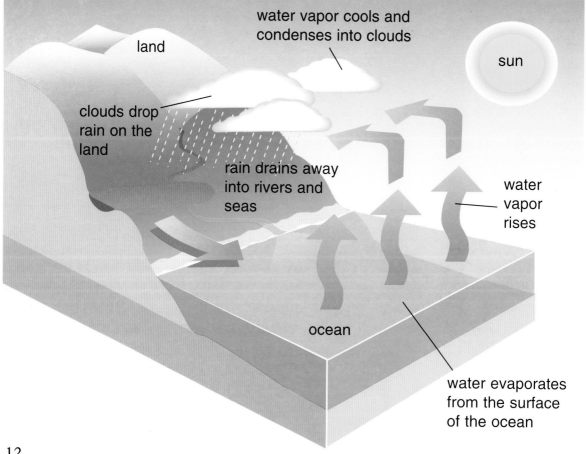

land

water vapor cools and condenses into clouds

sun

clouds drop rain on the land

rain drains away into rivers and seas

water vapor rises

ocean

water evaporates from the surface of the ocean

Winds pick up water vapor as they blow over warm oceans. When the winds reach land, hills or mountains may force the air currents upward. High in the air, water vapor cools and turns into clouds and rain.

Rain-bearing winds called **monsoons** cross the Indian Ocean to soak southern Asia. Monsoons are like sea breezes, but they occur seasonally instead of daily. Monsoons are much more powerful than sea breezes.

Monsoon winds bring heavy rainfall to most islands in Indonesia. The wettest months are December through March.

WIND FORCE

We can estimate the force of the wind by looking at its effect on smoke, water, or trees.

In 1805, a British naval officer named Francis Beaufort drew up a scale of wind forces, rated from 0 to 12. During the 1900s, three extra numbers were added to describe the severe storms called **hurricanes**. The Beaufort scale is still used to give people an idea of wind speed. The Beaufort scale defines words such as **gale**, but it isn't a very accurate measure of wind speed.

Antarctica is one of the windiest places on earth. The wind speed there may reach 200 miles per hour.

The Beaufort scale was first meant for use by ships at sea. It is also used on land. The chart below shows the first nine wind ratings.

The Beaufort Scale			
0	calm	0–1 mph	sea like a mirror, smoke rises straight up
1	light air	1–3 mph	smoke drifts slightly, seawater ripples
2	light breeze	4–7 mph	wind felt on face, leaves rustle
3	gentle breeze	8–12 mph	twigs move, flags flap
4	moderate breeze	13–18 mph	small branches move, dust and paper are blown around, waves form at sea
5	fresh breeze	19–24 mph	small trees move, waves form on lakes
6	strong breeze	25–31 mph	large branches sway, sea foams
7	near gale	32–38 mph	whole trees sway, walking gets hard
8	fresh gale	39–46 mph	twigs break off, sea foam is blown inland
9	strong gale	47–54 mph	roof tiles and branches are blown down

Scientists who study the weather are called **meteorologists**. They use instruments called **anemometers** to record wind speed. One type of anemometer has cups that catch the wind and whirl around and around. The fastest surface wind ever recorded was 231 miles per hour. It was measured at Mount Washington in New Hampshire in 1934.

Force 0

Force 2

Force 4

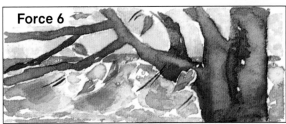
Force 6

Force 8

Force 9

See for Yourself

- Look for telltale signs of wind speed. Figure out where the wind fits into the Beaufort scale.
- Keep a record of wind speed each day for two weeks.

BLOWING HOT AND COLD

When cool winds rush in to replace warm, rising air, the temperature drops. In warm lands, people welcome a cool wind after a long period of hot, sticky weather.

In icy lands, wind can make cold air feel even colder. This effect is called **windchill**. For instance, a wind speed of 25 miles per hour can make a temperature of 32 degrees Fahrenheit feel like 1 degree. Sweating in cold weather makes us feel even colder.

Places that catch the full force of the wind, such as mountainsides, can become very cold.

Musk oxen live on the icy plains of the Arctic, where there is little shelter from the wind. Their bodies are protected by thick fur, which is covered by long hair.

Air currents that blow from warm regions or deserts raise the air temperature. One type of warming wind is called a chinook. After a rain-bearing wind drops rain as it climbs over a mountain, the chinook brings dry, warm air to the other side of the mountain.

In North America, chinooks sometimes roll down the eastern slopes of the Rocky Mountains. They can raise winter temperatures on the North American prairies by 30 degrees in less than an hour. The warm wind melts the winter snow.

LOCAL WINDS

Different types of winds blow in certain areas. The season, landscape, and weather conditions can all affect wind.

The Harmattan is a dusty, cool wind that blows south from the Sahara Desert. It crosses no seas or lakes, so it stays very dry. The Brickfielder is a hot, northeasterly wind that carries dust across Australia in summer months.

The Harmattan creates a dust storm in Mali, a country south of the Sahara Desert.

The Sirocco churns up waves as it blows north over the Moroccan coast.

The chilled air that flows from mountains down to valleys or the coast is called a katabatic wind. In Antarctica such winds whip up the snow and the waves.

The Sirocco blows north from the Sahara Desert into Italy and southern Europe. It starts out as a warm, dry wind, but it picks up moisture as it crosses the Mediterranean Sea.

WIND ON WATER

A strong wind can whip up the surface of the ocean and large lakes. Winds break the crests, or tops, of waves, making rows of whitecaps. Bubbles of air mix with the water to make spray and foam.

The wind makes most ocean waves. Tides, ocean currents, and underwater earthquakes also create waves on the ocean.

Whirling winds can be so powerful that they raise **waterspouts** from the surface of seas or lakes.

Whitecaps mark the crests of waves as they roll in toward the cliffs of Victoria, Australia. The distance over which a wind blows is called its **fetch**. The longer the fetch, the bigger the waves.

The distance from the top of one wave to the top of the next is called the wavelength. Each wave depth is about half the wavelength. As the water grows shallower near a coastline, the waves crowd together before they break. Water, wind, and pebbles are all churned up on the shore.

Strong winds may drive waves inland, causing flooding. Huge waves may batter the coast, wearing away rocks or pushing sand to another part of the coastline.

See for Yourself

- Fill a bowl with cold water. Let it sit until it is completely still.

- Blow across the surface. What happens?
- Where do waves have the most impact? Why?

SAND AND ROCK

Some deserts are like oceans of sand.
The wind may whip up twirling columns
of air called dust devils. Some winds raise
sandstorms, filling the air with dust that
can block light from the sun.

The wind blows loose sand into great banks
called dunes. Many dunes never stop
moving, shifting 200 feet or more each year.
The force of the wind forms dunes into
shapes such as crescents and pyramids.
It makes ripples on the surface of the sand.

The world's biggest
sand dunes are found
in the Sahara Desert.
Many dunes are 300
feet high and may be
many miles long.

In the deserts and canyons of Utah, the wind has carved rocks into strange shapes.

Desert winds can carry stinging grit made of bits of a sparkling rock called quartz. The grit wears down other rocks in a process called **erosion**. Particles of rock are worn away, and they form new grains of sand.

The wind carves soft rocks into strange shapes, such as arches, flat-topped tables, and towering pinnacles.

See for Yourself

- This camel lives in the deserts of central and eastern Asia. How do the following features help the animal survive in harsh winds and sandstorms:

- A thick shaggy coat?
- Thick eyelashes?
- Broad feet that spread its weight over a large area ?
- Padded feet?
- Nostrils that can be shut?

WIND AND PLANTS

Plants often grow in windy places. Their roots keep them from blowing over. Some trees, such as oaks and hickories, may grow roots that go 100 feet down into the ground.

The taller and wider a plant, the greater its **wind resistance**. Many mountain plants hug the ground or grow in cracks to reduce their exposure to the wind.

Coconut palms have thin, flexible trunks. The tree trunks bend over in strong winds.

When the wind blows, these catkins (parts of a birch tree) may release about five million grains of pollen.

Dandelion seeds float like parachutes. The wind helps spread the seeds far and wide.

Many flowering plants need the wind to spread their **pollen**, which are dustlike grains used in reproduction. The wind blows the grains from one plant to another. This is how plants make seeds.

The wind also spreads plant seeds. Small, light orchid seeds float in the air. Maple seeds whirl through the air like helicopter blades. The wind blows tumbleweed plants along the ground, scattering seeds as they go.

25

RIDERS OF THE WIND

Many birds spend most of their lives flying in the wind. Their **streamlined** shape helps them to slip through air with little resistance.

Air flowing beneath the bird's curved wing brings an upward force, keeping the bird aloft. To gain more height, the bird flaps its wings. This action helps the bird defy the force of **gravity**, which is tugging it down.

The kestrel is sometimes called the windhover. The bird seems to hang in the sky as it searches for prey below. By turning into the wind, the kestrel gains **lift**. It angles its wings and tail like a kite to catch as much wind as possible.

This huge seabird is a wandering albatross. It needs a powerful lift from the wind just to take off. It lives in the Southern Hemisphere in a region called the Roaring Forties. There, powerful westerly winds blow nearly all the time.

The big condors of South America use thermals, or rising currents of warm air, that help them soar above the mountains. Coastal birds fly with the help of sea breezes and the rising air currents near high cliffs.

Some birds **migrate** around the world. They fly with the help of global air currents such as the trade winds. The Arctic tern migrates more than 12,000 miles between the Arctic and the Antarctic regions.

Migrating birds, such as these Canada geese, take routes known as **flyways**. Flyways follow the prevailing winds and offer places where birds can rest and feed. A sudden gale may blow birds far off course.

DEADLY WINDS

Winds bring rain to dry places, but they can cause trouble, too. They may spread forest fires, uproot trees, and damage smaller plants. After such natural disasters, trees and plants soon grow back again.

Winds spread flames through the Amazon region in Brazil. The air currents feed the flames with oxygen, which aids the process of **combustion**, or burning.

Mount Pinatubo, a volcano, in the Philippines, erupted in 1991. It blew ash high into the atmosphere. Within three weeks, winds had carried the ash all around the globe.

Other disasters are not natural. Chemicals from factory chimneys or those used to spray crops may **pollute** the wind. In 1986, dangerous **radioactive** material escaped from the Chernobyl **nuclear power** station in eastern Europe. The winds blew radioactive dust westward as far as Italy, France, and the British Isles.

The wind also carries smoke, gases, and exhaust fumes. These substances mix with water droplets in clouds. The water then falls as **acid rain**.

Acid rain fell on this forest in the Czech Republic, killing the trees.

29

GLOSSARY

acid rain   Rain polluted by chemicals in the air

air pressure   The force of the atmosphere pressing down onto the ground

anemometer   Any instrument used to measure wind speed

atmosphere   The layer of gases around a planet

carbon dioxide   A gas found in the earth's atmosphere. Humans breathe it out, plants breathe it in

clockwise   Turning in the same direction as the hands of a clock

cold front   An advancing mass of cold air

combustion   Burning or catching fire

environment   Living conditions or surroundings

equator   An imaginary line around the middle of the earth

erosion   The wearing down of soil or rock by wind, rain, frost, or waves

fetch   The distance over which a wind blows

flyway   A route that migrating birds follow regularly

front   The border between two different air masses

gale   A wind that reaches speeds between 39 and 54 miles per hour

gas   An airy substance that fills any space in which it is contained

gravity   The force that pulls objects to the earth

hurricane   A storm with winds measuring more than 74 miles per hour

isobar   A line on a weather map showing places of equal air pressure

jet stream   A fast, high wind that circles the earth

land breeze   A breeze blowing from land toward water

lift   An upward force that allows aircraft and birds to take off and stay in the air

meteorologist   A scientist who studies the weather

migrate   To make a seasonal journey in search of food or breeding grounds

monsoon   Seasonal, rain-bearing winds that cross the Indian Ocean

nitrogen   An invisible gas that makes up most of the earth's atmosphere

nuclear power   Energy made by changing the structure of atoms

oxygen   A life-giving gas found in air and water

poles   The most northerly and southerly points on a planet

pollen	Tiny grains that enable flowering plants to reproduce
pollute	To poison land, water, or air with chemicals
prevailing winds	The most common winds in any region
radioactive	Giving out a dangerous type of energy
sea breeze	A cool breeze blowing from water toward land
streamlined	Having as little wind resistance as possible
temperature	Warmth or coldness, measured in degrees
troposphere	The part of the atmosphere nearest the earth
water cycle	The ongoing process in which rain falls, evaporates, rises, and condenses
waterspout	A whirling wind that forms a pillar between a cloud and water
water vapor	A gas created when water evaporates
weather	Atmospheric features such as heat, cold, sun, rain, and snow
windchill	The cooling effect of wind combined with a low temperature
wind resistance	The force with which objects withstand the wind

INDEX